In Sunshine and In Shadow Collection II

Poems of a Paranormal Nature

Dennis W. Carroll

Paralina Publishing

Cover photo by Dennis W. Carroll
Cover design by Brandon Hudgens
Book design by Brandon Hudgens

ISBN: 978-0-9898020-8-6
First Printing: August 2015

Nor was I now upon the trail,

Descending to that long-dead vale.

Around was fog—ahead, the spray,

Of star-streams in the Milky Way...

There was no hand to hold me back,

That night I found, the ancient track

- H. P. Lovecraft

Contents

Introduction

The Storyteller

At This Time of Night

Shadows of the Night

Late One Night

The Shadow of the Night

Skinwalker Wind

Bigfoot's In My Backyard

Dark Is The Night

Zombie Cowboy

The Ghost Breaker

Mr. Poe

Monsters of the Dark

Out There In The Night

Ghosts of Space

"It"

The Watcher

Never-Land

Moonrise (The Werewolf)

The Dark

She

The Door

Monster of the Mind

In A Dark Room

Uncounted Miles

Dark Things

Graveyard Dust

Night Wind

Wendigo

The Great Unknown

The Lady In White

A Knife in the Back

For Catherine

Ghost Wolf

The Girl On The Bridge

She Waits

Lost In The Shadows

The Monster Inside

Ghost

Whispers of the Night

The Wolf is at the Door

Lord of the Shadows

Mystic Night

Ghost Light

Dark Road

The Hour of Three

The Ghost

Vampire

Ghost of a Memory

I Will Rise Again

Into the Black

The Play

Left Behind

Somewhere In The Night

On The Wings Of The Night

The Game

Dark Dreams

Empty Rooms

Doorways

The Fairest Rose

Deal With The Devil

Isle Of The Dead

Dance With The Devil

Children of the Dragon

Going Down

In The Rain Tonight

The Road Unseen

Dark Angel

The Rising Dark

Tales of the Dark

He'll Come Knocking At Your Door

Necromancy (Demonic Reanimation of the Dead)

The Seven Sisters

Vanished

Rising Up From The Dead

Haunted House

Hunt The Night

Men In Black

The Graveyard Shift

The Witch

The House

Something Dreadful

Shadows

It's Out There

The Haunted Woodland

Dark Windows

Voodoo Moon

Cool Air

Nevermore

The Ghost of Johnny Ringo

Holes

To Be God

Resurrection

Demons

Eternal Love

The Lonely Grave

Windy Nights

The Shadow

The Hunt

It's A Strange Universe

To Thy Own Self Be True

Dream's End

The End

Introduction

Although this second volume of poetry is inspired in part by such masters of the macabre as Poe and Lovecraft, it has also been my career in the paranormal that has played a significant role in its inspiration as well. There is, of course, more of Shadow within this volume than Sunshine when it pertains to the subject matter at hand. The paranormal can sometimes be a strange and unsettling place of darkness and the unknown. A dim and dark land often seen very much in the shadows, where nothing may ever really be what it seems. However, we should also note that most of the time, you would not have shadows without the light. But what of those shadows born not of light? As Shakespeare would say..."There's the rub"... Come with me now, down that dark road, into those shadows and let us see, what we may find…

- Dennis W. Carroll

The Storyteller

The stories live on and the stories must be told...

Let me awaken the memory,
Of the days of old...
When time was free,
And the sun was gold...
When the nights were as dark,
As the tales that were told...
By the light of the fire
When the night wind grew cold...
Then late in midnight's lonely hour,
When the face of the moon is pale...
Gather closer to the fire,
And listen well...
Hold fast to the words,
And break not their spell...
For there are legends left to speak of,
And stories still to tell...

At This Time of Night

This is definitely a paranoid viewpoint, but in this case it may well be justified.

The wind moans as if weeping,
The moon rises cold and bright.
Sidewalks all are sleeping,
At this time of night...

Moving shadows on the wall,
Things just out of sight.
Who knows what may come to call,
At this time of night...

Midnight at the window knocks,
Only darkness beyond the light.
It might be best to check the locks,
At this time of night...

Strange noises at the door,
The clutch of fear so tight.
The evening now offers something more,
At this time of night...

Terror now seems at hand,
Is this the hour of your flight,
Or will you make your final stand,
At this time of night...

Will you face your fears unknown,
Will you flee or will you fight.
It's a thousand years till dawn,
At this time of night...

Shadows of the Night

Haunted by dark knowledge...

At the close of every day,
When the hours lose their light.
I try to keep, the darkness at bay,
and fight the shadows, of the night...

It's a battle that I cannot win,
With just a lonely circle of light.
Against the void, dark as sin,
and the demons, of the night...

I have learned more than most,
of the things that no one should know.
It is there, like an ever present ghost,
I am haunted by knowledge, learned long ago...

So I will keep this my lonely quest,
And pray for each dawn's early light.
the dark, an uneasy, unwelcome guest,
for I know what's really out there, in the night...

Late One Night

This was inspired by a very strange dream that I had once. I found myself walking at night on a long desert highway in this phantasm and was offered a ride, which I refused...

Late one night on a long lonely road,
Miles and miles, from anywhere...
Stranded in an deserted and desolate place,
With just the wind and the cold night air...

Your car is broken beyond repair,
No service on your phone, what rotten luck.
You walk this godforsaken black road,
and hope to see, another car or truck...

Then headlights approach on the horizon,
Slowly you see, a long black limousine.
It slows to a crawling stop where you stand,
The back window lowers, on this scene...

From out of the darkness of the backseat,
You hear a strange, male voice suavely say.
It's a bad night to be about in this country,
You can ride son, if you're going my way...

Then you see the eyes shining in the dark,
And a smile there too, colder than the night.
You've heard that voice before somewhere,
Everything here, just doesn't seem right.

I don't think so you hear yourself firmly reply,
This stranger, you now know only too well.
I've gone your way for too far too long,
Sadly I'm no stranger, to the highway of hell.

I've turned my footsteps to a higher path,
As you can see, I'm going the other way you say.
The smile is gone and the window goes up,
As the car slowly leaves, to vanish away.

Further on up the road you shake your head,
At the many masks, that he wears to hide.
Give him an inch he'll take the whole road,
Especially, when the Devil offers you a ride...

The Shadow of the Night

What if there was a spirit of the night itself and it stalked you to this end?

I've seen it in the darkness,
In the absence of the light.
At the edge of reality,
Is the shadow of the night...

It has a form like no other,
How can I ever hope to fight.
A wisp of smoke in the wind,
That is the shadow of the night...

I know it's coming for me soon,
It's waiting just out of sight.
It will collect me late one evening,
Then I will be the shadow of the night...

I will seek you in the darkness,
In the absence of the light...
I will wait at the edge of reality,
For I am the shadow of the night...

Skinwalker Wind

This is my take on those strange winds we may find ourselves in sometimes. Especially those that blow only ill winds and bad trouble...

There's a skinwalker wind,
Blowing tonight...
From out of the desert,
Where there is no light...

Bad things are borne,
On the dark breeze...
Out in the cold,
In the shadow of the trees...

Evil echoes off the canyons,
Of rock and of stone...
If you must travel tonight,
Don't go out alone...

On the outskirts of town,
Strange things are about...
Weird shapes with claws,
Fangs and a snout...

There is a darkness that stirs,
Where the shadows bend...
Don't get lost in the night,
Of the skinwalker wind...

Bigfoot's In My Backyard

This one was strictly for fun.

I saw Bigfoot, in my backyard tonight...
He was lookin for, a UFO,
With a big ole flashlight.
This neighborhood, used to be good...
But now it just ain't right...
Outer-space aliens and Bigfoot,
are In my backyard tonight...

There are Devil dogs and Zombies,
What an awful sight...
And the ghosts in my house are howling,
When I turn out the light...
And I hear chupacabras growling,
At old Bigfoot,
In my backyard tonight...

Mothman, was over by the trash can,
And he was helping his self...
I called some paranormal hunters,
But they got skeered and left ...

The men in black, are coming back,
I know they'll be here soon...
They will hypnotize, with their weird eyes,
And tell me it was a weather balloon...

What's a fella got to do,
But hide and turn out the light...
Sure Ain't gonna get no sleep...
With Bigfoot,
in my backyard tonight...

Dark Is The Night

There are some nights that seem much darker than others.

There's a bad wind blowing out there,
In the shifting shadows of the night...
Dark spells have been whispered,
Nights like this, will dim the light...

I can feel the darkness in the air,
Something unnatural has turned out...
Evil things now stalk the twilight,
In the shadows moving, all about...

Be wary of your way this night,
If you should find yourself alone...
For there are things in the blackness,
Of the shadows, that follow you home...

Whatever you do just stay inside,
Light a candle and say a prayer...
For the Devil walks abroad tonight,
And demons, have left their lair...

Hear the banshee wind wailing,
Feel the coldness of it's bite...
Dark is the night outside your door,
Make sure that you, should lock up tight...

Find yourself the brightest corner,
And indeed stay there till first light...
Until these things return to hell,
And go back into, that eternal night...

Zombie Cowboy

Why do we never see this type of Zombie? I'm sure he's walking because he ate his horse...

He's a walking dead, on the range,
From far down in Texas way...
As zombies go, he's mighty strange,
Don't get, in this cowboy's way...

He's been dead, for quite a while,
And he sure ain't gonna win no race.
But he's still got, a rather nice smile,
On that torn up, zombie face...

Southern zombies know, hospitality well,
They're deep fried that way so they say.
They will treat you right, and really swell,
And eat your guts, in a very nice way...

So if you chance, one night to see,
A zombie cowboy just like that.
Take this piece, of advice from me,
Whatever you do, don't touch his hat...

The Ghost Breaker

No comment...Mr. Hope...

If things get supernaturally out of hand,
You don't need to call a thrill seeking faker...
Don't need those guys from pest control,
What you need, is a real ghost breaker...

Ghost breaking is my specialty,
I'm not only a ghost hunter it's true...
I don't just find them you see,
But I will also, get rid of them too...

If a ghost is giving you a hard time,
And Devils are deviling you after all...
If there's a hidden treasure to be found,
Get in touch with me, and make the call...

So if you've got a haunted house,
Or maybe a howling ghost or two...
Here's my card just call me,
And I'll break a ghost, for you...

Mr. Poe

And now some questions for the Master of the Macabre...

Mr Poe...We need to know...
What was the reason of this woe...
This depression black as a raven,
Was it some dark pain long craven,
Deep within your shadowed soul...
We need to know...Mr Poe...

Did it follow you like a black cat...
A shade behind wherever you were at...
Was it the ghost of love lost long ago,
That gave your heart and spirit woe,
We wonder if this could have been so...
Now we'll never know...will we Mr Poe...

Monsters of the Dark

There is an old story that warns us not to stay too long in the dark or face grave consequences...

If you travel in the heart of midnight,
Do not go without a lighted spark.
For in the shadows born without light,
Abide the monsters of the dark...

None have ever lived to tell,
Not after the screaming starts.
The dreadful fate in which they fell,
And the fear that stopped their hearts...

Never stay for very long it's said,
In the shadows black as coal.
Some things will just make you dead,
And some things will eat your soul...

Some are never found again,
Some are found dead without a mark.
But they all wish they had never been,
found by the monsters of the dark...

Out There In The Night

This one tries to capture the feeling of a nightmare...one that becomes all too real...

Out there in the night...
In a place where shadows live...
Far from any feeble light...
That the evening, will not give...

You walk in the waiting quiet...
In the moonlit haze among the trees...
And where the path runs by it...
You feel the whisper, of the breeze...

There is something here with you...
Somewhere down the lonesome track...
Following close behind its true...
In the shadows, at your back...

In the darkness of your mind...
Feeding on your growing fear...
The footsteps now just behind...
You cannot deny, you plainly hear...

Will you turn to face what you deem...
is born in the shadows of your fright...
Or will you just simply scream...
And go running out, into the night...

Will you realize when you reach home...
That your fright was all in vain...
the sounds were echoes of you own...
Your imagination, takes the blame...

As you now go to unlock your door...
Your fears once more will come to abide...
To find what you thought fate had in store...
Is now waiting patiently, for you inside...

Ghosts of Space

This has to do of course will alien abduction, a truly fascinating aspect of ufology...

Beings with eyes, as black as the night,
From an unknown timeless place.
So the visit always goes,
With the ghosts from space...

Beyond the eternal, endless void,
From a forgotten shadow race.
Through the star flung doorways,
Of time and dark space...

They will always seek you out,
There is no place that you can hide.
They will feed upon your fears,
and the darkness, that lives inside...

They are waiting now for you to sleep,
In the misty dark an otherworldly face.
Near the bed and over by the door,
Are the ever waiting, ghosts of space...

"It"

This is dedicated to Cryptid Researchers everywhere...

What are those marks, on the ground,
Something's been here, is it still around.
Did you hear that weird and eerie sound,
It's out there, but it just won't be found.

Red eyes are watching, out in the trees,
There's a scent of something, on the breeze.
It may cause your blood to up and freeze,
When You hear it walking, in the leaves.

Way out in the dark woods, far from town,
better watch out, when the sun goes down.
It knows exactly where you can be found,
It may be time to head out, homeward bound.

The Watcher

And for those brave hearts who venture out on paranormal quests...
Bigfoot may also be looking for you...

In the night where shadows are many,
and lights are way too few....
Somewhere in the windswept darkness,
baleful eyes maybe watching you....

In the moonlight of the night,
Out in the brush and down in the canes..
Mankind has always known this creature,
by many different names.....

Some have caught a quick glimpse,
Footprints and signs on the ground...
and out among the trees a scent in the breeze,
When crickets quit and there is no sound......

Show this legend of the forest respect,
If you foolishly venture into it's domain,
And if you should mysteriously disappear...
you've got only yourself to blame....

For deep in the heart of the dark woods,
Something lurks just out of sight.
It maybe waiting for you in the shadows,
For Monsters, still walk in the night....

Never-Land

For the Peter Pan inside us all...

I will follow the second star to my right,
And straight on until the morn...
Across the valley of the night,
To where the dawn is born...

I seek such a land or a place,
Where one will never grow old...
Beyond life's common race,
There is such a place I'm told...

Where magic dust is very real,
Where one can fly upon the winds...
Where a Captain's hook is made of steel,
Where childhood in never-land never ends...

Beyond life's common race,
There is such a place I'm told...
I seek such a land or a place,
Where one will never grow old...

Across the valley of the night,
To where the dawn is born...
I will follow the second star to my right,
And straight on until the morn...

Moonrise (The Werewolf)

And now to unleash the beast...

I hear the call of every shadow,
Just beyond the pale moonlight.
Drawn to the darkness I must go,
One of the children of the night...

I go now where I've gone before,
Into the blackness that I must wander.
To feel again the animal roar,
Where body and soul are torn asunder...

To be one again with the night,
Is the spell that holds me still.
And once more by the moon's light,
I will go on the hunt to kill...

Now to stalk where shadows abide,,
Following ever close behind.
I use the spirit of the night inside,
For the prey that I must find...

Free at last I run alone,
Without care and without fear.
The hunger of blood drives me on,
To follow the chase far and near...

Soon in the wind there is a hint,
Of the coming of the dawn,
As I catch the morning scent,
That rises from the wooded lawn.

As star dials turn toward morn,
The night has shown me what can be.
Again I will know nature's scorn,
For once more I must put on humanity...

But the change will always find me,
The beast within is coming soon.
And I will break the chains that bind me,
With the rising of the moon...

The Dark

Darker than the darkness...

The spell is cast, the curse is spoke,
There is no end for what they start.
The force, of the darkness to invoke,
They call your name, from out of the dark...

In the deepest, of the darkest night,
Your fears will find their waiting mark.
Far forever, from the redeeming light,
Your fate is waiting for you, in the dark...

You cannot run, nor can you hide,
From these shadows black and stark.
They wait within, they wait outside,
They are waiting to find you, in the dark...

Pray for your safety, pray for your soul,
Light a candle against this devil mark.
Fear the falling night, as black as coal,
And look for the red eyes, in the dark...

She

A haunting ghost...

She was everything I ever wanted,
She was all and everything to me...
She will haunt me throughout all my days,
She is a ghost that will never set me free...

She is forever the owner of my heart,
She is the past that leaves me bereft.
She is always in my nightly dreams,
She is the memory of all that I have left...

She is now the debt I gladly must pay,
She will be the fate to which I shall bend.
She and I have forged an eternal love,
She is my beginning and She is my end...

The Door

Another ghost of the past...

In a dream I saw her again last night,
She could mend everything that was broke.
Our eyes locked and once more it was right,
She stayed to haunt me even after I awoke.

I live now only for such haunting dreams,
Alone I walk these sad forsaken halls.
Searching for lost happier days it seems,
Here where never again her footstep falls.

Come to me then my angel of the night,
Let me hold you in my arms once more.
Together we will walk into the waiting light,
And over the threshold of eternity's door...

Monster of the Mind

What makes us human monsters...

You can run all you want,
From the shadows behind....
But down your dark road,
Waits the monster of the mind....

It is with you from youth,
Till the day that you expire....
It is the darkness of your soul,
and the demon of your desire......

It hides behind your face,
The mask that you wear....
It is the beast of your Heart.
That waits in its lair.....

You may pray for its death,
only sadly in the end to find....
That you are a slave to your,
Monster of the mind...

In A Dark Room

I've been in a lot of dark rooms...

Outside in the lonely night,
The wind wails with banshee moans...
The storm has reached its wild height,
As it walks among the tombstones...

Along the wide and darkened hall,
Wait the windows that give no light...
The open door seems to call,
And you are drawn beyond all fright...

The hands that now reach out for you,
Are they but dark shadows unkind.
What is false and what is true,
What in this dark room will you find...

Why are you in this awful place,
Is it here at last you meet your doom..
The ghosts of your fears to face,
In this cold and dark room...

This room is there for a brave few,
And always in it you will find...
The fears that are there belong to you,
And they wait in the shadows of your mind...

Uncounted Miles

That unknown something out there that's watching...

Uncounted miles,
from an unknown mark...
Soulless black eyes,
Watching from the dark...

From the vastness of the void,
beyond time and space...
In the fears of endless night,
Terror will wear this face...

These things are never what they seem,
Behind the masks that they wear...
They are much less than a dream,
And far more than any nightmare...

As pale as the frost of death,
From out of the night black as coal...
They will await your final breath,
Perhaps to take from you, your very soul...

Dark Things

Some other things also out there...

There are things that walk this Earth...
things that don't belong....
Shadows that the darkness may birth.....
where evil has a throne....
Beware the dark shadows of the Earth....
for this is cast in stone....
the laughter of the Devil's mirth....
means that you, are never alone....

Graveyard Dust

More than the dust from which we came...

One day they will cover you with earth,
Deep down beneath a little mound.
And Soon the story of your life,
Will not even be found...

The love and the money we fought for,
That we thought would be ours in the end.
Will sadly forsake us on that day,
Like graveyard dust in the wind...

We will come to the ruin of forsaken glory,
Like The machines of man that rust.
Time will lay us all down low,
But we are more than graveyard dust...

Far past the gold and the sin,
Beyond the blood and the lust.
The soul within will rise again,
from out of the graveyard dust...

Like the unseen wings of angels,
Put your faith in a God you can trust.
For somehow deep down you must know,
We are much more, than graveyard dust...

Night Wind

What bad dreams are made of...

The cold moon looks down,
On the shadows of the town,
While the quiet night is sleeping...
Dreamers toss and frown,
and Midnight will softly drown,
In the darkness, that is slowly creeping...

Out among the grave stones,
The wind stirs and moans,
there is something moving in the night...
Leaves rattle like the bones,
That lie in their dark homes,
and there is a glimpse, of something white...

The restless cease to snore,
Awake they dream no more,
All sleep is brought to a sudden end...
They are startled to the core,
Was that something at the door,
Or could it have only, been just the wind...

Best to return to fitful sleep,
Down beneath the covers deep,
And worry not at what the hours may send...
What may be in the night will keep,
Where the darkest shadows creep,
Try to tell yourself, it's only just the wind...

Wendigo

The Native American Indian legend...

He is made of shadow,
Born not of the light.
He is all of your fears,
That stalk you in the night...

Of all that there is,
Above and below.
Beware my child,
Of the dreaded Wendigo...

He is a ghost of the land,
Older than time.
He kills out of hand,
Without reason or rhyme...

A hungry spirit of nature,
Here before man ever came.
He is the great unknown,
Made of darkness without name...

He can wear any face,
He overcomes in the end.
And your soul will be lost,
To the Wendigo wind...

The Great Unknown

What lies far beyond the unknown?

The time soon must come,
I know not the day or hour.
When Death will tally my sum,
and I will bow, to his power...

With my body beneath the clover,
I will then seek the other side.
With one single step over,
I will cross, that great divide...

At the end of the game,
Of me all that one will find.
A stone with just my name,
Is all that, I will leave behind...

The restless soul of the heart,
When the spirit of life is flown.
Will be forever now just a part,
Of the vast and great unknown...

I know not what awaits,,
At the river by the throne.
But when I pass through the gates,
I will at last, forever be home...

The Lady In White

Why should spirits linger...

She is a phantom of the moonlight,
A shadow beyond the veil of death...
She waits in the darkness of the night,
For The Lady in White has never left...

Is she waiting for someone to return,
Where her shadow no longer falls...
Her true fate we may never learn,
Or why she still haunts these halls...

Sadness is her only story to tell,
Is she looking for the stairway so bright...
Or is this a lonely and endless hell,
For the lovely lost Lady in White...

A Knife in the Back

I think we've all known a few folks like this...

There are those who will give you a smile,
Who swear a friendship that will never lack.
And declare a loyalty, but all the while,
They will leave a knife, sticking in your back...

Not all snakes crawl on the ground,
This is a clear and well known fact.
Some are false friends that walk around,
This truth is as real, as a knife in the back...

So beware of those who lie and deceive,
They are an evil poison ugly and black.
And don't ever let yourself come to believe,
they would never give you, a knife in the back...

For Catherine

I called her "Cat"...

As the years go slowly by,
Your memory grows clearer...
like our love it will never die,
With time it only grows dearer...

I look for you every where I go,
something is forever missing now...
My thoughts live in days of long ago,
I live on through it all somehow...

We will be together again my love,
Somewhere beyond the veil...
Far past the lonely stars above,
Where we will never again say farewell...

Ghost Wolf

This is for the Cherokee blood in me...

Somewhere between the worlds,
A spirit shadow stalks...
In the darkness of the night,
The white ghost wolf walks...

Guardian of the land and it's people,
The glory of days gone by....
He is a Son of the great spirit,
His stars are in the sky...

Ghost wolf have you lost your place?
With the children of the moon...
Once among us but found no more,
Are you gone so soon?

They dance to bring you back,
For days gone by they yearn...
But will we see your spirit again?
Will your magic ever return...

The Girl On The Bridge

My homage to a very famous ghost story...

Cars slow to cross the bridge,
and sometimes in the night,
someone will be waiting there,
just at the edge of the light....

Her skin is very pale,
her eyes are dark and deep,
there is a coldness about her,
that speaks of the final sleep...

But if you should give a ride,
To the girl with the long black hair,
when you reach your destination,
You will find she is not there...

For the girl on the bridge,
Time stopped long ago,
She has no place left in this life,
She walks a path of woe...

She is waiting for you on the bridge,
As if she has somewhere to be,
but her place is not in this world,
Only in the shadows of eternity...

She Waits

Lonely are the ghosts...

Late of a summer's night,
When the wind is in the trees.
And a full moon hangs high and bright,
Throwing shadows to the breeze.

There will come a scent in the air,
Of roses...All around.
It is then I know that she'll be there,
Without a trace of a sound.

Standing in the silver moon beams,
That linger in her raven hair.
A green eyed shade to haunt my dreams,
Is waiting for me there.

She is waiting for me always,
Calling for me in the night.
Through the ever darkening haze,
Where night birds take to flight.

And when the moon hangs no longer high,
As to the west it faces.
She and I will answer the echoing cry,
Of the lonely windswept places.

Soon the dawn will come to be,
But kind are the fates.
For with the night again she will come to me,
For me alone...she waits...

Lost In The Shadows

All is lost, without control...

Lost in the shadows,
We will play our part.
Lost in the shadows,
To the darkness of the heart...
I see the need in your eyes,
what the body can never forget...
I feel my blood begin to rise,
as we cast aside all regret...
Lost in the shadows,
lost to these dreams...
Lost in the shadows,
nothing is ever what it seems...
The night will be what it must,
love and lust are in our power...
Tomorrow may go down to dust,
tonight we live within this hour...
Lost in the shadows,
far beyond the light...
Lost in the shadows,
lost forever in this night...

The Monster Inside

The monster that's always there...

In passing strangers on the street,
Sometimes with a smile you greet.
You never know without a care,
What lies within, you'd best beware...

No matter what you may try,
Your nature you can never deny.
Nor can you ever hope to hide,
The monster, that lives inside...

The mirror shows what it can see,
In shadows too of what may be.
But the creature that is always there,
Is waiting within, it's human lair...

Always waiting to be set free,
To break the chains of humanity.
The enemy of all that is good and true,
Is the monster inside, that is really you...

Ghost

A nod to Poe's Spirits of the Dead...

From out of the darkness,
That extinguishes not The flame.
from the shadows of eternity,
I have heard you call my name.

From far beyond the black gulf,
across the wide and great divide.
Through the veil of life and death,
I stand once more at your side.

For love is stronger than the grave,
And true, true love never dies.
It is made of the fabric of forever,
That we've known in each others eyes.

So I will be with you always,
For with love, death cannot abide.
Until the end of your days my love,
I will be here by your side...

Whispers of the Night

Haunting memories...

There are whispers in the wind tonight ,
Darkness dances in the storm.
the fire has burned to ashes,
the coals are no longer warm...

I look deep into the shadows,
I hear something call my name.
my days are haunted by the past,
Now nothing will ever be the same...

I know My name is written in blood,
On a list in the reapers hand.
Now I must find the strength somehow,
To make my final stand...

Again I hear my name called,
In the whispers of the night.
There is something in the dark,
Something waiting just out of sight...

She comes to me from out the shadows,
I know her name is destiny.
And I know at last that is was she,
That was calling for me...

So I rise to take her hand,
She and I will take our flight.
together into the shadows,
To answer the whispers of the night...

The Wolf is at the Door

Dark days are fast upon us...

Through the mists of time we see them,
Long foretold in days of yore.
The age now has come to free them,
Now ride the bold horsemen four...

With a bow he bends to conquer,
armies on every shore.
In false armor he shines white,
But the wolf is hidden no more...

Comes a horseman of red,
Bloody is his blade with gore...
Smoke and fire cloud close behind him,
He is followed by the dogs of war...

Darker than the blackest night,
He is pain in a hungry place.
The rich fear not the black rider,
Only the poor shall know his face...

Pale Death rides forth at last,
Hell follows behind his horse.
The destiny of man is past,
His fate to run its final course...

Heed now the hour is growing late,
Cold winds and shadows upon the floor.
We all will share in this dark fate,
For the wolf is at the door...

Lord of the Shadows

The Father of lies...

Hear the wheeling bats whisper low,
Deep in the blackness of the hour...
Hear the wind's forsaken cries of woe,
Now that daylight has lost its power...

I am all that you have ever feared,
I am coming for you in the night..
The Master of horrors reared,
In the shadows born without light...

I am the Father of Hell's door,
I am the Prince of the power of the air...
I am the Bloody Captain of all war,
And I let loose the dogs of despair...

I am the darkness that follows behind,
Haunting you till your final breath...
And always keep this close in mind,
There are some things that are worse than death...

The throne of God is still my goal,
My battles are fought in midnight meadows...
I am the true enemy of your soul,
I am the Lord of the shadows...

Mystic Night

A strange night indeed...

I see your eyes in the stars of the skies,
I feel again your sweet touch so light.
in the heart there is a love that never dies,
It is ours again on this strange night...

I will wait for you in the moonlight,
we will be together once more.
The shadows of this mystic night,
Will open our love's dark door...

Across the years you will come to me,
Where night shadows softly await.
I will follow you then to eternity,
For my days have grown cold of late...

I will meet you then in the moonlight,
All will be as it was once before.
In the shadows of this mystic night,
Deep in the purple light, that lover's adore...

Ghost Light

The famous and legendary Ghost Lights, of which I've seen a few...

Ghost light, Ghost light,
shinning in the night...
Ghost light, Ghost light,
Dark and dim and bright...

Ghost light, Ghost light,
Moving in the night...
Looking for a home,
Guided by a light...
Through a vale of tears,
Across forgotten years,
To a place beyond human sight...

Into that uncertain night,
Don't look... look away,
Bow your head and pray,
Or you may never see another day,
If you are led astray,
by the haunting, Ghost light ...

Ghost light, Ghost light,
Out among the trees...
Ghost light, Ghost light,
Swinging in the breeze...

Does it mark where an angel fell,
Or does it lead to a gate of hell...
Held by no human hand,
A phantom bound to the land,
When it comes in sight,
Do not follow it into the night...
Or you will be another tale,
That they will tell...
of the haunting ghost light ...

Dark Road

To face a future unknown...

One night deep in what seemed a dream,
I found myself on a long and dark road.
Whether by plan or infernal scheme,
This was the path that I now strode...

Long were the shadows black,
That lay fast there upon the land.
Mocking were the echoes given back,
By my footsteps on the strand...

Whispering were memory's ghosts,
That followed close in my wake.
They were my dark and haunting hosts,
In this place I could not forsake...

There my future stood before me,
In robes of black and scarlet sorrows.
bound fast in chains that I could see,
Was this spirit of all the lost tomorrow's...

The days that I did so foolishly waste,
The hours all gone beyond recall.
The gifts given now spent in haste,
The power of love lost in my fall...

Oh God that I could turn back time,
Then I might could bear this heavy load.
But I have met the forlorn destiny that is mine,
At the end of life's lonely dark road...

The Hour of Three

It is well known in the field of Supernatural and Paranormal research and investigation, that Three AM is the hour of the power of darkness...

Deep, deep in the dead of night,
When the forces of evil exalt their power...
Darkness will seek to overturn the light,
At the height, of the Devils hour...

Far from daylight is the witching time,
Demons thrive at the hour of three...
It is the darkest of the night sign,
So heed this rhyme, or it may overcome thee...

Pray then for the time past four,
When the light of dawn is soon to come...
When fair day stands at the door,
And darkness shall no more, fight the sun...

For when it seems so very forlorn and dark,
And all hope of light seems far away...
The Earth will always turn upon her mark,
Then will sing the lark, to greet God's bright day...

The Ghost

Memories of a ghost...

For fifteen short years I knew,
what heaven on earth could be...
But Now a sad fate untrue,
Has robbed me of you,
Now the shadows of hell
Follow me...

In what should be my happiest hour,
I lose my smile as I turn away...
my thoughts go to your bower,
Where you hold the flower,
I gave you on your burial day...

You were far past my dreams,
you were better than an angel could be,
But the end it seems,
Doesn't justify the means,
For When you died,
it took the best part of me...

The vow we took is still good,
I still wear this ring that you see,
Nothing my dear wife ever would,
Come between us if it could,
For I'm still married to the sweet ghost,
of your memory...

As the sun sets each weary day,
I spend the haunted hours in walking this floor,
Waiting for the darkness that will stray,
And that shadows that hold sway,
In the dreams when you will come to me,
once more...

We will dance again together my dear,
For tonight dark death is our host...
I will hold you so near,
And whisper in your sweet ear,
That it is you…who dances
with a ghost...

Vampire

We've all met a vampire or two...

In the evening wind's vesper,
She came to me in the night....
Enchanting eyes of sky blue,
and clothed in starlight.....

In beauty beyond equal,
A splendor without name....
She has awakened eternal desire,
And set fire to the flame.....

Oh let me know your sweet touch,
Your burning kisses of ember....
Let me feel the chill of your skin,
Teach my heart to surrender...

Take all that you need,
I will give my life to this night....
Then let me fade away with you,
Into the mists of the pale moonlight.....

Ghost of a Memory

Do memories have their own ghosts?

Like dreams that fade to mind,
And thoughts are often lost in kind...
The halls of memory leave much behind,
and all we have bound we will unbind...

Like a meteor shining bright,
streaking across the starlit night...
blazing with all its might,
Soon forever lost to sight...

So shall it be with me,
when at last time sets me free...
Gone forever to sadly be,
A swiftly forgotten memory...

I will be a shadow in the wind,
Where dark and light do bend...
A faded ghost that time must rend,
To this sad and bitter end...

I Will Rise Again

Deo Favente Resurgam...
(With God's Favor I Will Rise Again)...

In the blackest night,
And in the darkest hour.
The Lord will be my light,
My refuge and my tower....

In the days of my sorrow,
Like a storm driven bird.
I am given hope for tomorrow,
By the promise of his word....

From where I now stand,
I shall not be forsaken.
From his unfailing hand,
I can not be taken......

What foe can be my enemy,
What evil can abide.
For mine is the victory,
With The Lord at my side....

If I must fall to the dust,
Then at the end I will begin.
In this I will forever trust,
That with his favor, I will rise again.....

Into the Black

Some times we can encounter the darkest of nights...

What waits out there in the shadows,
In the misty darkness at your back.
The final outcome no one knows,
When you dare to go into the black.....

In the empty night you can hear the wails,
On the cold and bitter wind that blows.
Where there is no light only darkness prevails,
and such is the fate of many lost souls.....

Of all the horrors in the mind's vice,
No matter what they may really be.
The one that holds your heart in ice,
Is the terror that you cannot see......

Too soon to lie beneath a stone,
The hours of days gone so silently.
The years to make you forever their own,
and bind you in the twilight of eternity......

So run...run on into the night,
and whatever you do don't look back.
Let nothing now stop you in your flight,
For behind you is waiting the endless black.....

The Play

As Shakespeare said...all of life is but a play and we are but players upon that stage...

The darkness of my days approaches,
The shadow of the tombstone is across my path....
There's a cold and bony hand on my shoulder,
Behind me I can hear the ravens laugh.....

Shades of dreams haunt my hours,
Dark have been my thoughts of late.....
Death and I it seems have been but actors,
In this ever on going play of fate....

Nights are darker than ever before,
Strange are the shadows that twist and sway.....
Storms wait on the horizon where cold winds blow,
Dawn will bring only a dark and cloudy day.....

This veil of frost has fallen over me,
The years of life have all flown away.....
Death waits for me on the road ahead,
These are the final lines of my play.....

Slowly now the heavy curtain falls,
Upon this sad stage of tears....
The blood and the gold count no more,
Now it all belongs, to the lost years.....

Left Behind

A terrible fate is to be left behind...

I woke this morning with my pillow in my arms,
For a minute I thought it was you.
I look at this big empty bed and wonder,
Do you miss our love so true...

Do you miss the warmth in the darkness,
Now that you've found someone new.
Though time and the years stand between us,
Deep down I'll be longing for you.....

I'll be yearning for your sweet softness,
The happiness that was your embrace.
But the time that was ours is gone now,
The future without you to face...

Deep in the night will you remember,
Will I ever again cross your mind.
Or will you awake some morning,
With no trace of me left behind...

So many bridges burned and fallen,
The path we can never retrace.
Broken dreams beyond all repair,
Have left us here in this place...

Now your journey will continue,
With hope that the miles will be kind.
But you will walk into the years before you,
With no thought of the one left behind...

Somewhere In The Night

More haunting memories...

Memories whisper to me,
In cold night winds that blow...
They say that I have lost forever,
The girl that I love so...

In the rain the shadows fall,
From darkness into the light...
And the storms of life are gathering,
Somewhere in the night...

Somewhere in the night,
There is shelter from the storm...
Eyes that call to me,
And lips so soft and warm...
Somewhere lovers meet,
Somewhere hearts are light...
But loneliness will always call,
Somewhere in the night...

Long I linger in the shadows,
With the darkness and the rain...
All that's left are the memories,
And this ever present pain...

Somewhere do you lie alone,
When there are arms to hold you tight...
And a heart that still longs for you,
Somewhere in the night...

Somewhere in the night,
In the winds of the storm...
The memories will wait for me,
Where the pain is born....
Somewhere lovers meet,
Somewhere hearts are light...
But tears will always fall,
Somewhere...in the night...

On The Wings Of The Night

Dark is the shadow of Death as he enfolds with his dark wings...

In the wind whisper the shadows,
Voices of darkness and gloom....
On the wings of the dark night,
Death has entered the room...

In shield and with sword,
Mourns the brave knight..
Gone is his noble youth,
and fled is his might....

The days of sweet sunshine,
Are now gone far behind..
For Beauty and youth,
The clock of years will not unwind...

He has fought well and hard...
Against the darkness for the light....
But all must bow to the one who comes,
On the wings of the night.

The Game

Fate and Death love this game...they always win...

This chess game I play with Fate,
Is more than just a game....
For in the shadows the reaper will wait,
The loser at last to claim.....

The pieces I must move to and fro,
Are a play I have made before.....
But as the mounting odds may grow,
I'm afraid my luck runs no more....

And so the game winds down,
As my men fall upon the board....
And I realize with a dire frown,
I have lost far more than I could afford...

"Check Mate"says Fate with a smile,
As I rise from the table my fears to tame....
So I must leave to walk the final mile....
With Death, the only winner of the game.....

Dark Dreams

What is dream and what is reality?

Dark have been my dreams of late....
Darker still may be my fate.....
For I feel a hand now pauses to wait....
Ready to wipe clean, my written slate.....

So the shadows that I see....
Are the only ghosts that now haunt me....
The faded spirits of my true destiny....
The revenants of a future, that can never be.....

Death raises no glass to toast...
For now I'm but the shadow of a ghost....
The devils will all laugh and boast...
For I have become, what I have feared the most....

Dark have been my dreams of late....
Broken now is the written slate....
Only the shadows for me await....
The unknown now, holds my fate.....

Empty Rooms

I have found that empty rooms are never truly "empty"...

Somewhere in the shadows,
That are cast without light.
Somewhere down a lonesome road,
Upon a dreary night......

A banshee wind is blowing,
Through the valley of the moon.
In the dust the shades are rising,
and they only whisper gloom.....

Where ends the pathway here,
a house waits with open door.
It's memories are many,
it's glory days are no more....

The wind moans lost and lonely,
Round these walls of pale stone.
This haunted place has weathered,
Many a storm to stand alone....

In its shadowed halls I wander,
with only a candle flame.
That stands against the darkness,
To see what calls my name.....

I halt before a darkened mirror,
my destiny has come too soon.
For by this glass I finally see,
That I'm only ghost here in this room....

Doorways

What if one day you stepped through an unknown door and were never seen again?

Dark are the things that remain unseen...
Dangerous are doors, that are not what they seem...
Dim is the boundary of what is real and what is dream...
For that is where no one, will ever hear you scream...

Forsaken are they who have fallen in between...
They remain buried deep as if in some dark scheme...
They are far less than shadow and little more than dream...
Perhaps lost to a world where they will never, again be seen...

The Fairest Rose

To love lost beyond the veil...

In the hall of years dear lady,
There is a place where you dwell.
Where our love is forever a thing of legend,
The fairest of stories still to tell...

A thousand swords cannot sunder,
In death and time we will not part.
For our love was the finest flower,
That ever bloomed in the human heart...

There was a place of happiness,
The essence of love divine...
Where I once held you in my arms,
and knew that you were mine...

You have taken the better part of me,
But it was yours from the very start.
and now throughout the ages of eternity,
We two are one to never part...

Oh fairest rose that ever was,
Beyond the veil you wait for me.
Soon the tides of time once more will turn,
At last to set our love forever free...

Deal With The Devil

A deal to avoid...

Don't ever make a deal,
That's not on the level.
and whatever you do,
Never shake hands with the Devil...

He will start with a compromise,
It will feel good to give in.
But It's all a pack of lies,
In a race you can't win...

The Devil never plays fair,
Never follows any rules.
If you play with him beware,
It's always a game of fools...

He is good at what he does,
He's the master of deceit.
and to deal with the Devil,
Will end in ruin and defeat...

Isle Of The Dead

There is a certain something about cemeteries, in the dead of night...

To this city of marble, I have been lead.....
To this silent isle of ruin and rubble.
I fear not the places, of the dead,
Only the living, are given to trouble.....

Here the dead lie, quietly sleeping,
Waiting for a trumpet sound....
Here the dead, their vigil keeping,
Neath the mossy, moonlit ground.....

I seek not the voices, of the dead,
But I know the secrets of their stones.
Breath has gone, and blood has bled,
All that is left, is the dust of bones.....

But far past this grey, granite cold,
Far beyond this world of sod.
Lives lived and stories told,
Will live on forever, in the heart of God...

Dance With The Devil

This is inspired by a well-known tale of the southwestern regions....Some people never listen...

Mama told her it just wasn't right,
it was time for prayers and a candle to light.
Serena's smile like her dress was bright,
as she headed out for the dance that night.

Dance like the Devil,
on Sunday night.
Dance like the Devil,
when you know it ain't right.
dance like the Devil,
till the break of day.
Dance with the Devil,
while the demons play...

Religion ain't much when you want something more,
the tall dark stranger met her out on the floor.

As he took her in his arms, she seemed in a trance,
she looked deep into his eyes, as they began to dance.
Faster and faster, they moved to the beat,

She knew something was wrong, by the look of his cloven feet.
He held her with blazing eyes of fire,
as she gave herself over to dark desire...

You can dance with the Devil,
when you know it ain't right.
dance with the Devil,
and be lost in the night.
The luck of the Devil never runs that long,
you can only dance with the Devil,
till the end of the song...

As the crowd watched just before dawn,
a terrible shriek was heard and then it was gone.
A flash of fire and horrible smoke,
the crowd screamed and then they broke.

All that they ever found, there on the ground,
was a burned piece of Serena's dress.
It seems when your date is the Devil,
you'll go down like the rest...

Dance with the Devil,
in the pale moonlight.
dance with the Devil,
when you know it ain't right.
Dance with the Devil,
till the break of day.
but when you dance with the Devil,
there'll be the Devil to pay.....
there's always.....the Devil to pay........

Children of the Dragon

We all run into these on occasion...

Not all snakes crawl on the ground.....
Some like people walk around....
Their bite is deadly so beware....
the children of the dragon never play fair....
Keep an eye on the shadows stay out of the shade.....
and wherever you walk keep a hand on your blade....
Never forget, after you cut off a snakes head...
The serpent can still kill, even after its dead.....

Going Down

Bad lives come to bad ends...

Hello loneliness my old friend,
The door was open and you walked in...
Pull up a chair and stay awhile,
You can watch as I, go down in style....

Fate laughs just like a clown,
Too many bottles in which to drown...
Its a long way to the bottom I've found,
There's no way up, when you're going down....

Well the party's over my old friend,
The good times at last have come to an end..
Destiny has won the final round,
here at the bottom, of a hole in the ground....

The devil laughs as they lower me down,
no friends are here to even frown...
They will soon push six foot of ground,
And pack it down tight, when I go down....

And pack it down tight, when I go down....

In The Rain Tonight

Out there in the dark, there may be many kinds ghosts...

A steady rain is falling,
Like angel tears coming down....
In the night wind is heard calling,
The lonely ghost of a sound...

Across the empty years,
I hear once more her voice...
Lost in a rain of tears,
It leaves my heart no choice...

There are ghosts in the rain tonight,
Haunting memories that won't lie still...
They are shadows born of darkness and light,
And they leave behind a freezing chill...

If I could but turn back time,
I would take the love back once more...
But you took what was mine,
When you opened that final door...

Love is so sweet they always say,
But love can cut just like a knife...
I found out on the dreadful day,
When you took the best of my life...

The lonely rain will keep on falling,
In the darkness far from the light...
The shadows of memories are calling
For there are ghosts in the rain tonight...

The Road Unseen

This road is there, if we will only look for it...

Beyond the shadows of this life,
Beyond the darkness and the green...
The shade of another world is waiting,
Down, a road unseen...

This unknown land is always with us,
Just at the edge of our sight....
Some have the courage to go there,
Fearing not, to face the night....

Far past the boundaries of life and death,
Of what is real and what is dream.....
The answers lie waiting for us,
Somewhere down, this road unseen....

So let us go once more my friend,
to where the mysteries may gleam,
Beyond the light, into tomorrow,
Down, the road unseen...

Dark Angel

Death be not proud...

I want to die standing up on my own,
For death and I have met before.
Then let his bloody blade cut to the bone,
For the spirit will still rise once more.....

Your dark throne stands no longer,
Scales of justice pay the cost.
Be not proud you are not stronger,
For the final battle you have lost...

Black angel of the dark wings,
Your victory at last is gone.
With The solemn bell that rings,
The last funeral will be your own......

Shed not for me your lying tears,
Nor show to me your baleful eye.
For when we are gone with the dust of years,
It is the spirit that will not die......

So from the grave there is no surrender,
It does not end in the blood and strife.
A stone is left there to remember,
That here from death rises...eternal life...

The Rising Dark

The power of the dark is always dangerous...

Beyond what is known there is knowledge and power,
In a place far past what is real and what is dream.....
In the halls of darkness you will stand alone in your hour,
For there will be none there to hear you scream...

Then stand to the light with the star of your faith,
soon will come the turning of the darkest tide....
For the shadows of shade and of wraith,
Will fall to the one on the angel's side....

But there are some things that walk this Earth,
That were never meant to be here.....
and they have given unnatural birth,
to the dire darkness of our fear.....

Then be always on guard my friend,
at all times and on every hand....
For when the light of each day doth end,
Then the shadows of night will rule the land....

So heed the power of the rising dark,
Do not let the worst of evil seek your side....
The heart of your soul is its final mark,
For where there is no light, only darkness will abide....

Tales of the Dark

The original campfire stories...

By the camp fire's spark,
When the world was new.
they told stories of the dark,
and some legends were true.....

In whispers they told,
of things best left alone.
Of secrets the shadows hold,
and of horrors unknown...

Deep in your soul they abide,
The tales are still within you.
and somewhere deep down inside,
You know that the stories are true...

What waits in the dark,
Only the light can reveal.
Is it imagination's mark,
Or do you know it to be real....

He'll Come Knocking At Your Door

Never open that door...
Especially if it's the Devil knocking...

In the deepening of the twilight,
where bitter breezes are known to blow.
Angels of mercy will flee in flight,
from a terror that no one should know...

Then he'll come knocking at your door,
He will come for all you hold most dear...
Only then to give you so much more,
Of all that you will come to fear...

In the gathering darkness of this night,
When shadows dare to walk the land...
All hope will fade with the dying light,
and love will lose its last command...

Then he'll come knocking at your door,
and your soul will pay the cost...
He will take what no one can restore,
and you will be forever lost...

Necromancy (Demonic Reanimation of the Dead)

From a story who's moral is, never read spells out loud, from old books...

By the force of the shadows,
and the power of the dark...
By these whispered words,
and the magic mark...

By wind and earth,
By fire and ice...
I call you forth,
To live again twice...

And when the moon,
Comes up blood red...
It will be the time,
Of the rising dead...

From the Second Book of Shadows...
By Silas Blackwood and Found in the Novel <u>The Rising Dead.</u>

The Seven Sisters

Dedicated to my favorite constellation...

Seven sisters of the misty dark.
Standing high at the midnight hour.
Dark is their magic to find its mark.
Darker still, is their power...

You will see them riding high.
By the Devil moon's light.
Far up in the velvet sky.
On the Eve, of All Hallows night...

Look to see them then.
They are never hard to find.
The beauty of their spell to spin.
Will cast its web, over your mind...

Vanished

Every year in the United States alone, more than six hundred thousand people vanish. Many never to be seen again...

In the forest dark and lonely,
On city streets of concrete canyon.
As if snatched by an eerie force,
The face of the earth to abandon...

People here and then suddenly gone,
At a much ever alarming rate.
The mystery remains in question,
Of those vanished to an unknown fate...

They who are no longer here,
Call out across oblivion's empty space.
Let the unseen not be forgotten,
Somewhere they still hold a place...

So many gone as if into thin air,
What is hunting the human race?
We are still haunted by this question,
How can you vanish without a trace...

Rising Up From The Dead

Some things it would seem, just won't stay buried...

There's a lonely night wind humming,
In the leaves that rattle like dry bones.
In the darkness there's something coming,
From out among the grey tombstones...

Haunting memories of you still bind me...
The ghosts of things we've left unsaid...
They're coming back tonight to find me...
They're rising up, rising up from the dead...

I dread the setting of the sun,
This nightmare waits for me still...
No place to hide, no where to run,
From spirits rising, rising with the chill...

They say old memories never die,
Tonight I know it to be so true...
In the shadows I spy, the gleam of your eye...
The only ghosts here, are me and you...

Haunting memories of you still bind me...
The ghosts of things we've left unsaid...
They're coming back tonight to find me...
They're rising up, rising up from the dead...
Rising up...from the dead...

Haunted House

I've been acquainted with many such houses and they all have a story to tell, if you just listen...

In the night so dark, the air was strange.
The wind that blew, across the grange.
Stirred the branches, of the willows,
Whispered past, the silvered windows...

A house stands here,
against the coming gale.
If it could speak,
What stories would it tell...

Would it tell of things,
that remain unknown.
Of murder at midnight,
And screams at dawn...

Of spirits that walk,
It's bloodstained floor.
Doomed here to stay,
Forever more...

Leaning against the wind,
And the falling storm.
Here it waits for its end,
Forsaken and forlorn...

Now only the memories remain,
With their legacy of dust.
Where alas time and pain,
Have broken their trust...

So I leave you to,
your sad and lonely fate.
A doom that for you,
Now that no longer, may wait...

Haunted thing,
of wood and stone,
I have found only in you,
ghosts of my own...

Hunt The Night

And now for those who follow us into the shadows...

Deep in the heart of darkness,
Amid the shadows of shade and light...
When you must turn to an unknown path,
in search of what is out there, in the night...

Then we join that band of the brave,
Who seek the truth of what is right...
Those who know this longing of the soul,
The ones who dare, to hunt the night...

The mysteries will always call to us,
The allure of secrets just out of sight...
the unknown beckons to draw us to it,
And that is why, we hunt the night...

We seek the answers that drive us onward,
Beyond the boundaries of dark and light...
The faith of our quest will never waver,
We will be there, to hunt the night...

Men In Black

And now for the infamous MIB...

They are a mystery to many,
And they always use fear to attack.
They deal in dark secrets unknown,
These very strange men in black...

Where do they really come from,
What is their true dark intent.
Are they alien hybrids or demons,
Or agents from a shadow government...

Whatever it is they truly may be,
We know they are up to no good.
One day you may see them on the street,
And the sidewalks of your neighborhood...

If one dark night there's a knock at your door,
in your peephole there's an eye looking back.
Pray that it's not your time for a visit,
From the mysterious men in black...

The Graveyard Shift

We've all known those darkest and longest hours of all, just before the break of day...

In the dead hours of the night,
Long before the hint of dawn.
The most longest hours of all,
Are the ones you must face alone...

In the darkness of the shadows,
Light is always a welcome gift.
Especially when something unknown,
Is with you on the graveyard shift...

In the loneliness of the forsaken hours,
When you start to feel you're not alone.
There's something out there in the dark,
And the feeling chills you to the bone...

Then be on guard in all your ways,
Never for a moment let your attention drift.
And don't ever let yourself forget,
Strange things can happen on the graveyard shift...

The Witch

This one just won't lie still...

Late one dark and windy night,
At a crossroads, way out of town...
By the glow, of my flickering flashlight,
I watched them, as they put her down...

They buried the urn with her ashes deep,
We all each, in turn took a hand...
We put her down, but she will never sleep,
The most evil witch, to ever walk this land...

She was vile and full of demonic hate,
She swore by Satan, to die was not his will...
Dark was her heart, and darker was her fate,
And we all know, that she will never lie still...

So on some evil night dark and dim,
She may once more, walk this earth alone...
May Satan get, what's coming to him,
And the Devil, can have his own...

The House

I have walked through this dark house many times...

There is a place that haunts my dreams,
In my mind I have been there many a time.
It's a large dark house on a hill it seems,
In a wildly forsaken and desolate clime.

Tombstones surround it on that dark hill,
Among the tall grass and the tortured trees.
The evil wind that blows there is never still,
And the bats wheel about like dead leaves...

It's door is always open and waiting for me,
There's a hallway of shadows and dust.
I must enter to find what there is to see,
Into that darkness I walk where I must.

There is one room that I see in my mind,
It is the one I've come to seek most of all.
A place where the darkest of shadows bind,
Where waits the worst of fates to fall.

It will be waiting again for me tonight,
On that lonely and haunted hill so far away.
I will seek its secrets of darkness and light,
Until I'm pulled back by the breaking of day.

I know that some lonesome dark night,
I will journey there never again to return.
Lost forever in shadow and pale moonlight,
The mystery of this house at last I will learn.

Something Dreadful

Here deep and dark in a goblin land,
You roam where you have lost your way...
An unknown place of danger on every hand,
You find yourself far from the break of day...

Pale then rises the baleful moon,
Where all hope dies with shallow faith...
Night is lost in the shadows of gloom,
And you must walk the way of the wraith...

Here the shades will bend and twist,
With the kiss of the night's cold wind...
Your fears will all be there to insist,
That you have come to your safety's end...

Then in the dark where evil shadows sway,
Always keep this thought in mind...
That something truly dreadful along the way,
May be coming up, BEHIND...

Shadows

Something to think about...

Look closer, at the world around you,
It's not the only world, there to see...
There are many, hidden shadows it's true,
Not all is whatever, it really seems to be...

There are shadows, in our lives we deem,
That only a few, may come to know...
There are dark forces, at work unseen,
That you will find out, to your sorrow...

They are hidden well, behind life's drone,
Insidious and evil, is their secret aim...
And once this hidden, knowledge is known,
You will never again, be the same...

Uncover then, whatever it is you must,
Only the brave, will face the unknown...
But never forget, be careful who you trust,
For we fight more, than just flesh and bone...

It's Out There

But whatever it may be, it's coming...

Its out there waiting, somewhere in the dark,
I can feel it and I know, it's coming for me.
Late on some lonesome, windswept night,
It will finally get me, just wait and see...

Sometimes it wears a hat, and a trench coat,
Sometimes it's just, a shadow in the night.
Late one evening, I'll let my guard down,
Then I'll disappear, forever from sight...

Wherever I'm at, I always watch the door,
All my days now have, a much darker hue.
Nights are spent, fighting against this terror,
It'll come for me, then it'll come for you...

Oh yes it'll come for you, just wait and see,
When the moon is down, in the night so black.
There's nowhere to hide, no place to run,
To keep on living, you better keep looking back...
It's Out There...

The Haunted Woodland

A place I know only too well...

Dark in the shadow of the mountain,
Where icy cold waters flow...
Hard by a desolate forsaken fountain,
Where few will ever dare to go...

There in the shade of an ancient wood,
Waits a stark forest grim and old...
Here long forgotten ruins have stood,
Waiting for the adventurer bold...

Hear the howl of wolves on the breeze,
There is darkness on the path at hand...
And ghouls are seen among the trees,
In this strange and haunted woodland...

Do you dare walk this legendary place,
Where the sum of all fear is found...
Here where wild nightmares race,
Over this dark and bloody ground...

Here shadows may just be evil things,
where nothing ever really dies...
Night must soon take to her wings,
And wraiths seek their graves by sunrise...

Come then with me upon this dark trace,
to where this fog shrouded forest does stand...
The secrets here we will dare to face,
Deep in this haunted woodland...

Dark Windows

Dark windows are creepy things and I always look to see if anything is looking back...

Dark windows that look out into the night,
Dark windows always watching me...
Like deep black eyes that have no light,
Sometimes it seems they look into eternity...

I often stare into their depth of field,
In every old and abandoned place...
Wondering sometimes their shock to yield,
Perhaps to see looking back at me a face...

The feeling of being watched is strong,
I've stood by many dark windows you see...
Knowing always that something is wrong,
Looking to see what is looking back at me...

Dark windows can be like a evil dream,
Like nightmares deep and as black as coal...
For they are never really what they seem,
Windows are the eyes of the haunted soul...

Voodoo Moon

Another ballad of high adventure and black magic...

The moon that tropic night rode high,
Over the city of old New Orleans.
It looked just like a skull in the sky,
And we all know, just what that means...

It's means a dark night of evil you see,
And you know that it's coming soon.
For they are dancing with devils set free,
In the pale light, of a voodoo moon..

They sent Jean Claude to find me,
To pay with my life for some photos I shot.
I saw a dark ritual that no one should see,
They sent my friend, to kill me on the spot.

But Jean Claude had been buried for a year,
And It's hard to kill something that's dead.
Thank God my machete was close by and near,
It's never easy, to cut off a zombie's head.

In dreams those lifeless eyes will haunt me,
As I poured salt into that mouth of decay.
I made sure he was dead as dead could be,
I buried him with a bible, at the break of day.

There's a doll of me out there somewhere I know,
They whisper and chant over it as they twist and bend.
Black candles are lit as they wish me dark woe.
Casting their spells and cruses, for my terrible end.

Tell them in New Orleans I won't be back,
I've looked too closely at the face of doom.
And in the dark when shadows are black,
I will still hear the drums on the night,
of a voodoo moon.

Cool Air

My nod to Mr. Lovecraft and the Night Gallery...

I live for the season of winter,
I revel in the ice and the snow...
I dread the airs of summer,
And I'll tell you why, it is so...

I found a way to extend my life,
I've cheated death as my fate...
Winter slows my decomposition...
Summer however, accelerates the rate...

I've lived far past my years now,
I seldom venture far from my lair,
I am tied in the heat of summer,
To the machine, that gives me cool air...

I'm a slave to my mechanical master,
But if I can make it to winter again...
I will find where there never is summer,
And withdraw, from the world of men...

The price of love and immortality,
Is in the end never quite fair...
Will my lady love depart with me,
To where, we'll always have cool air...

So I wait for the end of warm weather,
With a fear that I cannot drown...
And I dread to hear the dying hum,
Of my machine, if it should break down...

Nevermore

Another nod to Mr. Poe...

Raven, Raven in the night...
Eternal eyes of blackest coal...
Raven, Raven on your flight...
To collect, the wayward soul...

Yes your name is Nevermore...
I know just why you've come...
You wait for me upon my door...
The destiny, I can't out run...

The darkness of death you are...
With a blacker heart at your core...
It seems just at the rising of my star...
You steal, my hopes once more...

Thing of evil thou devil bird...
From some demon haunted shore...
I see tomorrow die with that one word...
The haunting cry, of Nevermore...

The Ghost of Johnny Ringo

When you're the best, you always answer the challenge, no matter what and as Doc Holiday would say... "I'm you're Huckleberry"...

The word had gone out across the land,
That Red Ward wanted to give it a go...
He claimed the fastest draw at hand
He said he could take, Johnny Ringo.

That night it was quiet at the birdcage,
When Ringo came through the door...
He was looking for Red Ward to engage,
With a draw no one could see, they swore.

Then it was over and swiftly done,
With a single shot deadly and clear...
Red never cleared the holster with his gun,
Before Ringo made him pay, quite dear.

Then Ringo holstered his deadly friend,
Looked at the crowd silent and cool...
As he turned no one said a word to this end,
It was as quiet, as a Sunday School.

At the bat wings he stopped still as a frown,
Turned with a terrible look of strange woe...
He said, "I've got to go and lay down now,
Cause you see, I died three days ago".

Then there was nothing there at the door,
Not even the sound of a retreating horse...
Then we all quickly crossed the floor,
But there wasn't anything, to see of course.

We only heard the lonely wind that night,
Among the tumbleweeds out in the street...
Johnny Ringo was gone clear out of sight,
Never seen again, his maker at last to meet.

Holes

Some holes can never be filled...

We encounter many holes in our lives,
Some of which we never can fill...
Some it seems we are born to acquire,
And others over which we have no will.

But sometimes we foolishly dig our own,
With what we waste to chase our goal...
When things are worth more than people,
We end up with a hole for our soul.

The pursuit of Money digs the deepest,
Time we squander will take a deadly toll...
Self love will bury you so much deeper,
In the dark hole you dig for your soul.

Someday when your time has ended,
They will dig a place for you to be found...
It's true we all must go this way someday,
But they never put a living soul in the ground.

Yet there are some who walk among us,
Whose love for everything has grown cold...
They are walking dead and empty inside,
For their true soul has already been sold.

So my friend as these lines you ponder,
Be careful as the years of your life unroll...
The way they you treat others around you,
Can be the hole in which you lose your soul.

To Be God

It's always a dangerous game, when you try to be God...

In the night the wind was strange,
Blowing hard across the grange.
A clouded pale moon looked down,
On the graveyard just out of town...

Another one taken from the fresh earth,
Waiting for my science to give it rebirth.
Fools do they not know genius to see,
And what wonderful miracles soon to be...

Looking up at the lightening in the sky,
To capture its power I know I must try.
To bring up life from out of the cold sod,
To stand among men and know I am God...

Darker grows the night with the storm,
I leave for my place waiting and warm.
I look back at the graves and smile this time,
They will remember the name of, Frankenstein...

Resurrection

At the end of days...

Soon will come the time long foretold,
When the trumpets of God will sound...
Then will rise all the dead of the earth,
From where they sleep in the ground...

Those who rise up first are the happiest,
Their great reward will come to be...
But those who are raised up second,
Only know their damnation to see...

For that most important of all days,
The trumpets are now being tuned...
When some will know the glory of heaven,
others will know what it is to be doomed...

So with each dawn the earth is waiting,
To hear those clear trumpet sounds...
When comes the final day of resurrection,
Out in the old graveyard grounds...

Demons

To engage an ultimate enemy...true faith is the best weapon...

They always find me wherever I'm at,
Especially on the edge of nightfall.
These things that are made of the dark,
But they're not really shadows at all...

I've fought their kind before,
A battle that I must fight alone.
Against an enemy that will not die,
And is not made of flesh and of bone...

They are the darkness of this world,
They are often called demon by name.
They seek only our ultimate destruction,
They are insidious evil all the same...

One day I'll fall in this lonely battle,
The blood will stop at last in my heart.
But I will fight them to the very end,
To where the line of eternity must start...

Eternal Love

And yes, true, true love, never dies...

Know now that I love you my dearest,
You were the substance of my every dream.
And you are still part of my lonely heart,
Across space and time, it may seem.

I hear you cry at night by my grave,
I've stood by your side on many a day.
I watch over you now from beyond,
I'm still here for you, in every way.

I will not leave you ever my sweet love,
Not in sunshine or in the winter rain.
Till the day we're together once more,
And I can hold you, close to me again.

For when God makes two hearts into one,
He will see that they shall be one as before.
Two hands clasped forever together,
On some fair and distant, golden shore.

The Lonely Grave

Every gravestone has a story...

Out one day wandering all alone,
I found myself on a path unknown.
In a place that I had never seen,
A quiet glade, in the gentle green...

In its center stood a small tombstone,
Weathered, unmarked and all alone.
I paused at this symbol of silent grief,
And wondered at what, lay here beneath...

Was it a life well lived or one with pain only,
To end here sadly in this grave so lonely.
Given up at last to the earth's cold sod,
With a place now only, in the memory of God...

Was it someone's sweet beloved child,
Here laid with their dreams in this place so mild.
Or someone's faithful dog and sweet friend,
Here given to rest, at it's life's good end...

How very sad and serene it did seem,
I must tread softly for here lies a dream.
Quietly I turned and started for home,
And left that soft glade, to its lonely gravestone...

Windy Nights

When there's mystery on the wind...

I have come to love windy nights,
When it seems the whole world is alive.
The shadows that bend and move,
When the wild winds of evening arrive...

Anything could happen on a windy night,
Things move with a mystery all their own.
It is then that the veil is at its thinnest,
Beyond all that is dark and unknown...

When the midnight wind is blowing,
Sometimes I hear it call my name.
As if their were spirits on the breeze,
It is a call I must answer all the same...

So on some windswept starry night,
I will wander to face the darkness alone.
I will be found in the shadows of evening,
Far, far, from the warm lights of home...

The Shadow

A nod to true friendship and devotion...

There is a dark, black shadow,
That follows me wherever I go.
I can always be sure it will be there,
This is one thing, I can count on to know...

Sometimes across the room, I see it,
Intently watching and waiting for me.
My every move seems very important,
My steps are constantly, followed you see.

But this shadow, that relentlessly follows,
Is not one of black sorrow or dark woe.
It is one of undying love and devotion,
A friend who will follow, wherever I go.

A true friend, is my black Cocker Spaniel,
A really good little fellow named Zac.
We always look out for each other,
He's always on guard, for a monster attack.

So now it seems, I have two shadows,
One is my dog and the other my own.
My shadow is always a close part of me,
And the other will see, that I'm never alone.

The Hunt

The number one rule of hunting...

One windy night, when the moon was bright,
As I tracked something down a dark path...
I soon came to a stop, at a forty foot drop,
When I heard something behind me laugh...

I whirled around, but I stood my ground,
I heard a voice from the shadows then say...
What you hunt it's true, can also hunt you,
And that's why I can always get away...

Keep this in mind, always be looking behind,
I will without a doubt be watching you...
It's just the same, two can play this game,
I'll certainly be closely following you too...

I stood in place, with a red blush on my face,
I knew what this thing said was true...
I had been such a fool, forgot the first rule,
What you're hunting for can also hunt you...

It's always great, to search and investigate,
But remember for the rest of your days...
You can't ignore, hunting is just like a door,
When it's open it will always work both ways...

It's A Strange Universe

Never forget...

I've seen some amazing things,
In my few short years on this earth...
I've looked at demons one on one,
And shadows to which light gave no birth...

I've stalked the things that walk in the night,
And things unseen have left me with scars...
Felt the spirit chill of the supernatural cold,
seen something that blocked a sky of stars...

Many strange lights and unnatural things,
These and others that are just a few...
it truly is a strange universe out there,
And it's waiting for me and for you...

But we must do all to keep on looking,
Chasing mysteries to the edge of eternity...
Let's find out now what's really out there,
Join the hunt, come along and follow me...

To Thy Own Self Be True

It is as Mr. Shakespeare wisely once said...

I've seen some strange things in my time,
But the strangest thing of all to me...
Is how people can blind themselves to truth,
And see what only, they want to see...

As Shakespeare said wisely once long ago,
To thy own self you should always be true...
But some people see only what they want,
No matter what, is the true honest view...

See what only is really there plainly to see,
Set your own personal opinions aside...
When you see it clearly for what it really is,
Only then, should your decision abide...

For the biggest fool of all in this world,
Is the one that believes not his own eyes...
They deny what is plainly true and real,
They never look for the truth, where it really lies...

Dream's End

All dreams die and must conclude...

Here upon a memory haunted shore,
I stand among life's continuing roar…
All that I know now, I must finally deem,
Was but a dream, within a lonely dream.

Gone are days among the crowds alone,
Searching but never finding my real home…
Looking to quench, my heart's true desire,
The dream at last, consumed by that fire.

I look up to the starry Milky Way streams,
To see all that is left of all the dead dreams...
For bright meteors that are seen, by the eye,
Are but dreams headed to heaven, after they die.

Now through these final hours that are mine,
I bow to my enemy, my deadly foe time...
In my heart now only, blows a lonely wind,
Through its empty halls, to my dream's end...

The End

And this of course is where we end...

I have looked into the face of darkness,
And it has made me hold the light, that much more dear...
I have stood before the vast unknown,
And found that there was nothing left, for me to fear...

I have seen beyond the shadows of life,
Deep into that eternal night...
And I have found that waiting for me,
On the other side, there is a light...

Then I will happily come to the starry gates,
That will open when my time is done...
I will not look back for even a brief moment,
But I will finish the race that I have run...

Oh Death the enemy be not proud,
Your victory is only dust in the wind...
You cannot destroy what is not yours,
For the spirit lives on, far beyond the end...

"I stand amid the roar,
Of a surf tormented shore.
And I hold within my hand,
Grains of the golden sand...
How few, yet how they creep,
Through my fingers to the deep,
While I weep...while I weep...
Oh God can I not grasp,
Them with a tighter clasp.
Oh God can I not save,
One, from the pitiless wave...
Is all that we see or seem...
but a dream, within a dream"?

Edgar Allan Poe

The End